TRADITIONS AND CELEBRATIONS

HALLOWEEN

by Charles C. Hofer

PEBBLE
a capstone imprint

Published by Pebble, an imprint of Capstone
1710 Roe Crest Drive
North Mankato, Minnesota 56003
capstonepub.com

Copyright © 2024 by Capstone. All rights reserved. No part of this publication may
be reproduced in whole or in part, or stored in a retrieval system, or transmitted
in any form or by any means, electronic, mechanical, photocopying, recording, or
otherwise, without written permission of the publisher.

Library of Congress Cataloging-in-Publication Data
Names: Hofer, Charles, author.
Title: Halloween / by Charles C. Hofer.
Description: North Mankato, Minnesota : Capstone Press 2024. | Series: Traditions
    and celebrations | Includes bibliographical references and index. | Audience: Ages
    5 to 8 | Audience: Grades 2-3
Summary: "Halloween is a holiday that features all things creepy and scary! Also
    known as All Hallows' Eve, people enjoy decorating their homes with jack-o-
    lanterns, spider webs, skeletons, and other creepy items. Many kids love to dress
    up in costumes and go trick-or-treating for candy. Some people enjoy watching
    scary movies. Discover how this holiday began and the spooky ways people have
    fun with it."— Provided by publisher.
Identifiers: LCCN 2022050198 (print) | LCCN 2022050199 (ebook) |
    ISBN 9780756575656 (hardcover) | ISBN 9780756575601 (paperback) |
    ISBN 9780756575618 (pdf) | ISBN 9780756575632 (kindle edition) |
    ISBN 9780756575649 (epub)
Subjects: LCSH: Halloween—Juvenile literature.
Classification: LCC GT4965 .H578 2024 (print) | LCC GT4965 (ebook) |
    DDC 394.2646—dc23/eng/20221020
LC record available at https://lccn.loc.gov/2022050198
LC ebook record available at https://lccn.loc.gov/2022050199

Editorial Credits
Editor: Aaron Sautter; Designer: Jaime Willems; Media Researcher:
Rebekah Hubstenberger; Production Specialist: Whitney Schaefer

Photo Credits
Alamy: FALKENSTEINFOTO, 9; Getty Images: Dave Etheridge-Barnes, 7,
duncan1890, 6, Gerard Puigmal, 23, Jamie Garbutt, 15, Jose Luis Pelaez Inc, 19,
kokouu, 13, L Cranson/Transcendental Graphics, 10, Nikada, 24, Raymond Gehman,
8, Tais Policanti, 21, Yuya Shino, 26; Shutterstock: FOTOKITA, 18, Gorodenkoff, 29,
gpointstudio, 5, legenda, 14, mTaira, 27, Olinda, 25, Shandor, 22, Supamotion, cover,
Victoria Lipov, 16, Zulfiska, 1

Design Elements
Shutterstock: Rafal Kulik

All internet sites appearing in back matter were available and accurate when this
book was sent to press.

Printed and bound in China. PO5379

TABLE OF CONTENTS

TRICK OR TREAT! 4

HOW DID HALLOWEEN BEGIN? 6

HALLOWEEN TODAY 11

HALLOWEEN AROUND THE WORLD 20

GLOSSARY 30

READ MORE 31

INTERNET SITES 31

INDEX 32

ABOUT THE AUTHOR 32

Words in **bold** are in the glossary.

TRICK OR TREAT!

Ghosts and goblins. Black cats and witches. Candy and costumes. These are all part of the spookiest day of the year.

In the United States, Halloween is celebrated on October 31. It has many **traditions**. Some are old. Some are new. But all of them are fun. And there's always a lot of candy!

HOW DID HALLOWEEN BEGIN?

Halloween began long ago as a festival called Samhain. It was celebrated by the **Celtic** people. The Celts lived in what is now Ireland and England.

Druids were religious leaders for ancient Celtic people.

Samhain marked the end of summer. The Celts believed this was when ghosts walked the earth.

The Celts wore costumes during Samhain. They also had big **bonfires**. They believed the fires helped keep ghosts away.

The word Halloween comes from "All Hallow's Evening." This is the day before All Saints Day. This is an important day for **Christians**. It is a time to remember those who have died.

Some people visit graveyards on All Saints Day to remember the dead.

On All Saints Day, the poor would visit rich people. They might sing a song or perform a magic trick. In return, they were given bread and other foods. Some believe this led to today's tradition of trick-or-treating on Halloween.

Immigrant families brought Halloween traditions to America.

HALLOWEEN TODAY

Halloween as we know it started in the late 1800s. Many Irish **immigrants** moved to America. They brought the traditions of All Hallow's Eve with them.

But Halloween has changed a lot over time. Halloween is no longer a **religious** holiday. And there are many new traditions. Some are scary or spooky. Some are zany and fun!

Wearing costumes on Halloween is a lot of fun. People can dress up as scary vampires, spooky ghosts, or silly monsters. They can even pretend to be their favorite superheroes.

Kids love to go trick-or-treating. They visit people's homes in their neighborhood. When someone comes to the door, they shout, "Trick or treat!" Neighbors then give out candy.

It wouldn't be Halloween without jack-o-lanterns! People once believed these spooky carved pumpkins could scare off wicked ghosts and **spirits**. Today, making them is a fun and messy Halloween tradition for many people.

First, a hole is cut into a pumpkin. Then, the seeds are scooped out. Next, people carve a funny or spooky face in the pumpkin. Finally, people place a candle or lights inside the jack-o-lantern. Then, they put it by the front door. It's a fun way to say "Boo!" on Halloween.

Haunted houses are another spooky Halloween treat. Visitors enter through a creaky door. Inside, the house is dark and creepy. Shadows dance on the ceiling. A scary howl is heard. Then, something jumps out from behind a door! It's safe but scary fun when visiting a haunted house.

Decorations are also a big part of Halloween. Many people enjoy decorating their homes with cobwebs and jack-o-lanterns. Others set up fake spiders, gravestones, ghosts, and skeletons in their yards.

Halloween is a special time of year. Summer is over. The leaves are falling. It gets dark early, and a chill is in the air. It's a great time for scary movies!

Many people love watching scary movies on Halloween. They grab some popcorn and sit on the couch with friends. They like the thrill when something scary happens on the screen.

HALLOWEEN AROUND THE WORLD

Other countries celebrate holidays similar to Halloween. In Mexico, people celebrate *Día de los Muertos*, or Day of the Dead. It takes place on November 2. It is a time to remember family and friends who have died. Some even celebrate the pets they have lost.

People set up **altars** to honor the souls of the dead. The altars contain photos of people who have died. They also include the favorite foods and drinks people enjoyed in life. People say prayers at the altars so the dead will hear them.

Altars honor those who have died.

Day of the Dead is also about having fun! People celebrate this holiday with long **parades**. They often wear beautiful face paint and colorful traditional clothing. People also enjoy gathering at fun parties to give gifts and share candy.

Day of the Dead candy

Day of the Dead parade

Day of the Dead is celebrated in the United States too. It is very popular in places like Los Angeles, California, and San Antonio, Texas. These cities are home to many people from Mexico.

Countries in Europe like Germany and France celebrate a holiday like Halloween. It's called St. Martin's Day. This holiday marks the end of the harvest. It's celebrated on November 11.

People enjoy roasted goose dinners on St. Martin's Day.

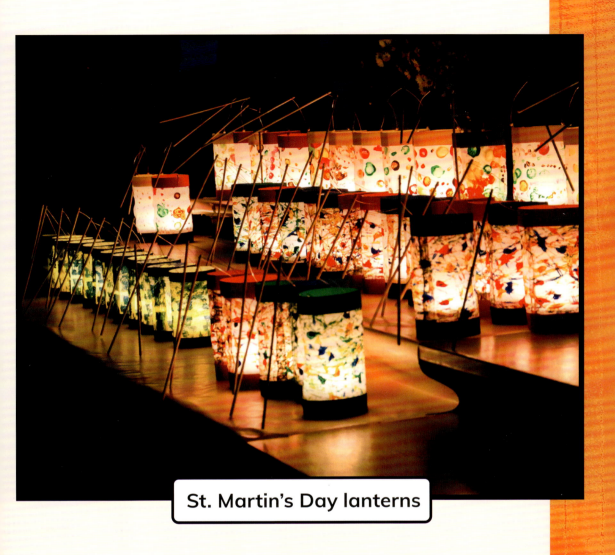

St. Martin's Day lanterns

St. Martin's Day is a time for a **feast**. It's also a day for a big party with friends and family. Children like to visit their neighbors. They carry lanterns and sing songs.

In Japan, people celebrate Obon. This holiday takes place in August. Obon is a time to remember family members who have died. People light floating lanterns and float them down a river.

Halloween is also becoming popular in Japan. It's celebrated much like it is in the United States. Many people love to dress up in costumes. They also enjoy Halloween parties, parades, and candy.

Obon lanterns floating on a river in Japan

Halloween is a fun holiday for the whole family. Wherever people live, they can celebrate Halloween.

Join your friends. Join your family. Wear a fun or scary costume. Carve a jack-o-lantern. Go trick-or-treating. Visit a haunted house or watch a scary movie. Halloween comes just once a year. So have fun!

GLOSSARY

altar (AWL-ter)—a special structure, such as a platform or table, where religious ceremonies are performed

bonfire (BON-fyre)—a big fire built outside

Celtic (KEL-tik)—having to do with the people and culture of Ireland and Scotland

Christians (KRIS-chuhns)—people who believe in and follow the teachings of Jesus Christ

feast (FEEST)—a large, fancy meal, usually for a lot of people to celebrate a special occasion

immigrant (IM-uh-gruhnt)—a person who leaves one country and settles in another

parade (puh-RADE)—a line of people, bands, decorated cars, and floats that travels through a town to celebrate a special event or holiday

religious (ree-LIJ-uhs)—having to do with a certain religion or one's spiritual beliefs

spirit (SPIHR-it)—a ghost

tradition (truh-DISH-uhn)—a custom, idea, or belief passed down through time

READ MORE

Bullard, Lisa. *My Family Celebrates Halloween.* Minneapolis: Lerner Publications, 2019.

Heinrichs, Ann. *Celebrating Halloween.* Mankato, MN: The Child's World, 2021.

Salazar, Alicia. *Día de los Muertos.* North Mankato, MN: Pebble Explore, 2022.

INTERNET SITES

Ducksters: Halloween
ducksters.com/holidays/halloween.php

National Geographic: Halloween Hangout
kids.nationalgeographic.com/pages/topic/halloween-hangout

PBS Kids: Happy Halloween
pbs.org/parents/halloween

INDEX

altars, 20, 21

candy, 4, 12, 22, 27
Celts, 6–7
costumes, 4, 7, 12, 27, 28

Day of the Dead, 20, 22–23
decorations, 17

France, 24

Germany, 24
ghosts, 4, 7, 12, 14, 17

Halloween history, 6–9, 11
haunted houses, 17, 28

immigrants, 10, 11

jack-o-lanterns, 14–15, 17, 28
Japan, 26–27

lanterns, 25, 26

monsters, 4, 12

Obon, 26

parades, 22, 23, 27
parties, 22, 25, 27

scary movies, 18–19, 28
St. Martin's Day, 24–25

trick-or-treating, 9, 12, 28

ABOUT THE AUTHOR

Charles C. Hofer enjoys writing books for young students. He's written many books about animals, culture, science, and sports for young readers to enjoy. Charles lives in Tucson, Arizona.